Homeowners' Guide to Maintenance

RYAN BRAUTOVICH

Copyright © 2012 Ryan Brautovich

All rights reserved. No part of this book may be reproduced or transmitted in any form or by any means, electronic or mechanical, including photocopying, recording, or by any information storage and retrieval system, without the written permission of the Publisher.

Printed in the United States of America

November 2012

ISBN: 978-0-9864404-5-8

"Less is more. I truly believe in buying a few pieces with better construction."

~ Stacy London

The Construction H.E.L.P. Foundation's Home Construction Audit program makes it easy and painless – through the use of our Home Building System – to understand how to build a home, how to manage your contractor, and how to protect yourself from being taken advantage of and scammed. We demystify the process and remove all of the contractor jargon to give you the building process in easy-to-understand, plain English. The Construction H.E.L.P. Foundation's founder and building expert Ryan Brautovich's exclusive 4-step home building system will ensure you are on the right track – and on budget – every step of the way. For more information about the Construction H.E.L.P Foundation, the Home Construction Audit Program, or any of the educational products, homeowner services, or construction seminars available in your area, please visit **www.HomeConstructionAudit.com**, or **www.ConHelp4U.org**.

TABLE OF CONTENTS

HOMEOWNER MAINTENANCE TIPS

Bathroom Caulk	1
Ceramic Tile Grout	1
Chimney Cleaning	1
Doors	1
Drains	2
Drywall	2
Electrical	2
Fencing	3
Garage Doors	4
Gutters and Downspouts	4
Insect Control	4
Irrigation Sprinklers	4
Locks	5
Sink Traps	5
Solid Surface Countertops	5
Trim and Siding	5
Vents	6
Water Heater	6
Windows (includes Patio doors)	6

ANNUAL HOMEOWNER MAINTENANCE LOG

Year 1	9
Spring Home Maintenance	10
Summer Home Maintenance	11
Fall Home Maintenance	13
Winter Home Maintenance	14
Year 2	16
Spring Home Maintenance	17
Summer Home Maintenance	18
Fall Home Maintenance	20
Winter Home Maintenance	21
Year 3	23
Spring Home Maintenance	24
Summer Home Maintenance	25
Fall Home Maintenance	27
Winter Home Maintenance	28

Year 4	30
Spring Home Maintenance	31
Summer Home Maintenance	32
Fall Home Maintenance	34
Winter Home Maintenance	35
Year 5	37
Spring Home Maintenance	38
Summer Home Maintenance	39
Fall Home Maintenance	41
Winter Home Maintenance	42
Year 6	44
Spring Home Maintenance	45
Summer Home Maintenance	46
Fall Home Maintenance	48
Winter Home Maintenance	49
Year 7	51
Spring Home Maintenance	52
Summer Home Maintenance	53
Fall Home Maintenance	55
Winter Home Maintenance	56
Year 8	58
Spring Home Maintenance	59
Summer Home Maintenance	60
Fall Home Maintenance	62
Winter Home Maintenance	63
Year 9	65
Spring Home Maintenance	66
Summer Home Maintenance	67
Fall Home Maintenance	69
Winter Home Maintenance	70
Year 10	72
Spring Home Maintenance	73
Summer Home Maintenance	74
Fall Home Maintenance	76
Winter Home Maintenance	77
BIBLIOGRAPHY AND REFERENCES	79

HOMEOWNER MAINTENANCE TIPS

The following list of minimum maintenance requirements that should be performed by the Homeowner along with a maintenance schedule. This work should be done either by the Homeowner or by a maintenance person who is experienced and insured. A maintenance person who holds a contractor's license is typically better qualified. Failure to adequately maintain the following areas may eliminate or reduce the Builder's Responsibility if a problem arises.

Bathroom Caulk. The caulk joints in bathrooms need to be inspected and re-caulked (if necessary) every six months. This includes the joint at the bottom of the shower, the joint between the tub and the wall, the joint where the tub or shower pan meets the floor, and vertical inside corners and seats. It is very important that these joints do not pass any water; otherwise dry rot can accumulate regress unseen for years. Joints should be cleaned of old caulk before re-caulking. Any mold or mildew found growing in bathrooms (or other places in the House) should be removed immediately with a mildewcide, available at most hardware stores. The cause of the mold or mildew should be discovered (for example a leaky window or failure to use vent fan while bathing) and the cause subsequently eliminated.

Ceramic Tile Grout. Re-grout or color caulk all cracks after the first year. Once the House frame reaches equilibrium (in less than two years), re-grouting or caulking should not be required. Tile grout should initially be sealed with a silicone based sealer and thereafter every two years.

Chimney Cleaning. The chimney flue should be professionally cleaned every two years if there are more than 50 fires per year or if there are more than 25 fires per year using wax and sawdust logs; subject to any restrictions or requirements of the manufacturer.

Doors. Patio sliding doors should have their tracks (bottom sill) swept and vacuum monthly. The weep holes should also be inspected and cleaned as needed. Dust and dirt build-up in slider door tracks will interfere with the proper operation of the small wheels that the doors slide on. For swing doors, the hinges and latches should be lubricated annually with a dry lubricant specifically made for locks and latches.

Drains

- **Deck.** Deck drains should be flushed with a garden hose and should show evidence of free-flow prior to the start of each rainy season.
- **Yard.** Yard drains should be flushed with a garden hose prior to the start of the rainy season and should show evidence of free flow at the curb or at the sump (if applicable).
- **Sub-drains.** If the House is equipped with a subterranean drainage system around the foundation or through the foundation, the cleanouts (if applicable) of this sub-drain should be flushed prior to the start of the rainy season. There should be evidence of free-flow through the curb or into the sump.

Drywall

- **Cracks.** Minor cracks in drywall usually appear within the first 12 months of occupancy. These cracks typically occur around door frames, cabinets, and window frames and can be easily caulked.
- **Nail Pops.** Nails will sometimes back out of the drywall as the frame of the House dries out. This is not a structural problem, but the nails should be re-driven and the heads should be spackled and painted with touchup paint.

Electrical

- **GFIs.** Ground Fault Interrupters should be tested monthly. When testing, pressing the black TEST button should cause the red or white RESET button to pop out. Push in the RESET button to restore the circuit. If the GFI will not reset, it may be faulty or there may be an open circuit. Contact a qualified, licensed electrical contractor to check the circuit.
- **Closet Ceiling Lights.** Light bulbs in the closets must be covered with a lens or globe as part of the fixture. When changing bulbs in the closet light fixtures, do not exceed the manufacturer's recommended wattage for the build requirement, and do not leave the fixture cover off. Lights left on in closets can generate a significant amount of heat and become a fire hazard.

- **Aluminum Wiring.** While most household wiring is copper, the larger wires (known as cables), are likely to be aluminum. All wires are covered with insulation. Aluminum cables are often used to provide power to air conditioners, heat pumps, electric clothes dryers, and electric ovens. Aluminum is a softer metal than copper. Over time it can deform, or "creep", where it is connected. When aluminum creep occurs, the connection is no longer tight and sparking jumps through the gap. Appliances will consume more power and breakers will trip. It is recommended that the terminal connections of aluminum cables be inspected and tightened if necessary by a qualified, licensed electrical contractor within the first two years after occupancy.

Fencing

- **Wood.** The condition of wood fences should be inspected every spring. Looks for nails that have backed out of boards, fence posts that are leaning and kick boards (at the bottom) that have rotted. All leaning posts should be straightened, all loose boards should be re-nailed and if the kick boards have rotted significantly, they should be replaced.
- **Wrought Iron.** Wrought iron gates and fences should be inspected four times a year to check for rust, particularly at the base of all posts. If rust is discovered, it should be scraped away and the section should be painted with rust-resistant touchup paint.
- **Stucco.** Stucco fencing (patio fencing), should be inspected annually, in the springtime. Cracks on the top of the fence should be caulked and repainted and fence post bases should be inspected or dry rot. All dirt should be removed from the fence post bases.
- **Furnace Filters.** If the House has heating and air conditioning, the furnace filters should be changed at least every six months or at the filter manufacturer's recommendation. If the House has heating only, the furnace filters should be changed prior to the winter season. If the Homeowner lives in an area that has considerable wind driven dust, the above filter change schedule should be doubled.

Garage Doors
- **One piece.** One-piece garage doors (doors that raise and lower one single piece) with automatic openers or garage doors without automatic openers should be lubricated at the hinge points every six months with 30w oil. The keepers (the long threaded rods that run across the top and bottom) should be kept tight to prevent the door from sagging in the middle.
- **Sectional.** Sectional doors (doors that roll up into the garage ceiling on tracks) should have the track rollers lubricated with 30w oil annually.
- **Automatic Opener.** The automatic openers, whether they are chain drive or screw drive, should have the drive mechanism (chain or screw) lubricated with a light grease annually.
- **Bolts.** Garage doors vibrate while opening and closing. Therefore, it is important that an inspection be made every six months for the first year and annually thereafter for bolts that can be wiggled or moved by hand.
- **Weatherstripping.** Check flexibility and contact with floor.

Gutters and Downspouts. Gutters and downspouts should be cleaned and flushed twice annually. The first task is performed just prior to the rainy season, and the second task is performed during the rainy season after the trees have shed their autumn leaves. Prune branches that overhang roofs and gutters..

Insect Control. Insects, particularly termites and carpenter ants, can be harmful to the structure of the House. An annual inspection should be made of the foundation (both on the outside and inside of the crawlspace). Look for brown termite tubes running up the foundation walls and bore holes of the carpenter ants on the exterior of the House. Builders typically do not warrant against any type of insect invasion. Homeowners should pay close attention to pest control maintenance and should not hesitate to call a pest control service if destructive insects are suspected to be present. Firewood should be stored away from the House in a structure or holder that is not in contact with the ground. Do not let vines grow on the House; they will attract insects.

Irrigation Sprinklers. Irrigation sprinklers should be checked annually at the beginning of the growing period (usually March or April) to be sure that the heads are clean and do not spray against the House and that the sprinkler lines have not broken during the winter. Spray patterns should also be checked during the growing season. During the rainy season, irrigation controller times should be changed frequently to avoid overwatering and flooding.

Locks. Once a year, or when they become stiff, apply a dry lubricant as directed into the lock. Use a lubricant specifically designed for locks and avoid use of popular oil synthetic sprays. The latter can form gummy residue on lock parts.

Sink Traps. Depending upon frequency of use, sink traps should be cleaned with a cleanser approved for the type of plumbing pipes under the sink (plastic or metal). For a kitchen sink that receives daily use, a cleaning every 60 days should be sufficient. DO NOT put sink cleaner into a garbage disposal. It may corrode the cutting blade edges.

Solid Surface Countertops. Do not apply countertop surface enhancers or cleansers such as Pledge or 409 to a new solid surface countertop. These products will only attract and hold discoloring items such as coffee, wine, catsup, etc. to the surface. The new nonporous, bacteria-free solid surface countertop will remain in its natural state if it is simply wiped off with a soft sponge or cloth, with an ammonia based product such as glass cleaner, or with a mild soap and water solution. For integral solid surface sinks, use milk abrasive such as "Softscrub" to cut any grease or discoloring buildup that has accumulated on the surface of the sink. Clean off any harsh chemicals such as nail polish remover as soon as possible. Do not cut directly on the solid surface countertop of slide a rough edged objects across the countertop, since these items will create surface scratches in almost any type of countertop. To prevent shocking the surface of any type of sink, do not pour extremely hot grease or water into any sink without simultaneously running cool water. Do not place extremely hot items (such as sheet pans from a 450 degree oven) directly on the countertop or sink.

Trim and Siding. The term "trim" refers to the wooden trim either abutting the stucco or placed on the wooden siding around windows and doors. The trim should be inspected each year prior to the start of the rainy season; and if the trim is pulled away from the House or the caulking has deteriorated, these areas should be re-caulked. If warping or twisting is severe (more than ½ in). the trim should be replaced. Do not caulk the bottom gap of the trim piece over a window or patio door. Also, the siding (exterior wall material such as panels, lap boards, shingles, or other non-stucco, non-brick, or non-stone material such as panels, lap boards, shingles, or other non-stucco, non-brick, or non-stone material) should be inspected for warpage and protruding nails. Inspections should be annual and prior to the start of the rainy season. Warpage should be caulked and painted, and protruding nails should be pulled and replaced with a slightly larger nail. Use hot dipped galvanized box or common nails in exterior applications. Drive the nail head even with the siding; DO NOT drive the nail head into the siding. Driving the nail head into the siding may break the seal and cause the siding to swell and leak during precipitation. Touch up all work with caulk and paint.

Vents. This includes kitchen hood filters and bathroom laundry fans. The hood filters should be removed and washed with a grease removing cleanser at least 4 times a year (depending upon use). Bathroom and laundry fans should be vacuumed with a hose vacuum and crevice tool at least once a year. Clothes dryer vents must be kept open lint free. Accumulation of lint will significantly reduce the efficiency of the dryer and, under some circumstances, become a source of fire in the duct. Depending upon the degree of use, and the length of the dryer duct, the dryer vent ducts should be cleaned every two to five years.

Water Heater. To prolong the life of the water heater, accumulated sediment should be removed from the heater tank once a year. This task can be performed by attaching a thick wall garden hose to the drain spigot at the bottom of the tank and draining out no more than two gallons. Since the water being drained is very hot, be very careful that the hot water does not come into contact with persons, animals, plants, or any material that could be damaged by scalding water (120 degrees F to 160 degrees F).

Windows (includes Patio doors)

- **Seals.** Inspect for broken or breached window seals in dual pane windows at least annually. Windows with broken or breached seals are easily identified by having a moist, foggy, or filmy condition between the two panes of glass. When this condition exists, the insulating value of the window is greatly diminished. The only repair is to replace the window.
- **Weep Holes.** The weep holes at the bottom of windows and patio doors serve a purpose: to allow water to drain out from the track during rainstorms. Weep holes should be inspected at least annually to make sure that no debris has plugged the holes and that rainwater will drain freely from them.

- **Tracks.** The tracks of windows and patio doors should be swept and vacuumed frequently to prevent dust and debris buildup. Clean window and door tracks, allowing the sliding vent to move more freely, so that the drainage through the weep holes will not be impaired by any wet debris. In open areas where there is ongoing construction or agricultural operations that generate dust, track cleaning should be done weekly.

ANNUAL HOMEOWNER MAINTENANCE LOG

Year 1

Spring Home Maintenance

In spring, focus on freshening up your home and protecting your property against the season's strong winds and rains.

Outdoor Tasks:

- ☐ Clean gutters, downspouts, and drains.
- ☐ Inspect roof and chimney for cracks and damage. Inspect all sheet metal – caulk and repaint as needed.
- ☐ Clean deck, patio, porch surfaces, and inspect for surface damage or loose fasteners.
- ☐ Touch up peeling or damaged paint.
- ☐ Check for loose or missing address numbers, or numbers obscured by trees or vines. Clean, paint or polish as needed. Trim or prune any plants covering the numbers or blocking the view from the street. Check numbers at night to verify operation of installed lighting (if any).
- ☐ Lubricate and adjust garage door tracks, rollers, springs, drive chains, screw rods, hinges, door panels, etc. Inspect garage door for scratches or damage, repaint as necessary.
- ☐ Inspect and lubricate gate hinges, latches and locksets. Repaint as needed.
- ☐ Door Chime operates properly.
- ☐ Wash all windows, inside and out.
- ☐ Install screens on windows and doors.
- ☐ Clean outdoor furniture and air out cushions.
- ☐ Service your lawn mower.
- ☐ Irrigation is operational and adjusted to not spray the house.
- ☐ Fertilize your lawn.
- ☐ _____
- ☐ _____
- ☐ _____
- ☐ _____
- ☐ _____

Indoor Tasks:

- ☐ Test smoke and carbon monoxide detectors when you set clocks forward.
- ☐ If your basement has a sump pump, test it by dumping a large bucket of water into the basin of the sump pump. This should activate the sump pump. If it does not switch on or if it's not pumping water, it may need to be serviced by a professional. Also, check for and remove any debris and make sure there are no leaks.
- ☐ Wash and change seasonal bedding.
- ☐ Dust blinds and vacuum curtains throughout your house.
- ☐ Clean kitchen and bathroom cabinets and throw away outdated food, medicine and cosmetics.
- ☐ Inspect and re-caulk any area in kitchen and bathroom where dissimilar materials meet (bathtub-to-tile, toilet-to-floor, sink-to-countertop, etc.) and separation has occurred.
- ☐ Inspect all plumbing fixtures for leaks.
- ☐ Check all porcelain fixtures for cracks.
- ☐ _____
- ☐ _____
- ☐ _____
- ☐ _____
- ☐ _____

Summer Home Maintenance

In summer, complete the following projects to keep your yard lush and your home cool.

Outdoor Tasks:

- ☐ Walk around your home's exterior and slide open crawl space vents at the foundation.
- ☐ Prune trees and shrubs.
- ☐ Inspect and lubricate mailbox hinges, latches, and locks. Paint as needed.
- ☐ Inspect for pests and wood destroying organism activity.

- ☐ Remove lint from dryer exhaust vent with a long, flexible brush.
- ☐ Uncover central air conditioner and install window air conditioners.
- ☐ Inspect gas meter and pipes for rust and corrosion. Remove rust, prep and paint as necessary.
- ☐ _____
- ☐ _____
- ☐ _____
- ☐ _____
- ☐ _____

Indoor Tasks:

- ☐ Change or clean heating, ventilating and air conditioning filters. Consult manufacturer instructions for your furnace to determine whether you need to change filters more frequently. Learn more about choosing a filter.
- ☐ Clean kitchen appliances inside and out, including refrigerator coils.
- ☐ Maintain clean drains by adding a half-cup of baking soda followed by a half-cup of white vinegar. After 10 minutes, flush with boiling water.
- ☐ Drain or flush water heater.
- ☐ _____
- ☐ _____
- ☐ _____
- ☐ _____

Fall Home Maintenance

In fall, prepare your home and yard for cooler temperatures, falling leaves and more hours spent indoors.

Outdoor Tasks:

- ☐ Clean gutters and downspouts.
- ☐ Water flows freely away from house and does not pond excessively on patios, decks, porches, etc
- ☐ Inspect roof and chimney for cracks and damage.
- ☐ Inspect all attic block vents, roof vents and gable end vents to verify that the screens are intact ant that no debris is blocking the screens. Replace any missing or damaged screens.
- ☐ Check for loose or missing address numbers, or numbers obscured by trees or vines. Clean, paint or polish as needed. Trim or prune any plants covering the numbers or blocking the view from the street. Check numbers at night to verify operation of installed lighting (if any)
- ☐ Rake leaves and shred to use as mulch or dispose of them based on local guidelines.
- ☐ Close or install storm windows. Clean tracks and lubricate locking hardware, rollers, etc. Be sure weep holes in windows are clear, and free of debris (if applicable).
- ☐ Remove hoses from spigots and drain and store indoors, coiled and flat.
- ☐ Store outdoor furniture and cushions.
- ☐ Test snow blower and have it professionally serviced if necessary.
- ☐ Rake Leaves
- ☐ _____
- ☐ _____
- ☐ _____
- ☐ _____
- ☐ _____

Indoor Tasks:

- ☐ Test smoke and carbon monoxide detectors when you set clocks back in the fall.
- ☐ Check windows and doors for weather-tightness and install weather stripping where it's needed.
- ☐ Have furnace professionally inspected.
- ☐ If needed, set traps for rodents.
- ☐ Dust blinds and vacuum curtains throughout your house.
- ☐ Clean kitchen and bathroom cabinets and throw away outdated food, medicine and cosmetics.
- ☐ Inspect and re-caulk any area in kitchen and bathroom where dissimilar materials meet (bathtub-to-tile, toilet-to-floor, sink-to-countertop, countertop-to-backsplash, etc.) and separation has occurred.
- ☐ Inspect all plumbing fixtures for leaks.
- ☐ Check all porcelain fixtures for cracks.
- ☐ _____
- ☐ _____
- ☐ _____
- ☐ _____
- ☐ _____

Winter Home Maintenance

In winter, enjoy energy-efficient warmth and the fruits of your home-maintenance labors. Use this time of the year to thoroughly clean and care for your home's interior while taking a few precautionary measures on the outside.

Outdoor Tasks:

- ☐ Walk around your home's exterior and check the crawl space vents located at the foundation. Close any that are open.
- ☐ Protect your central air conditioning unit with a cover, and remove and store window air conditioners.
- ☐ Clean and store garden tools.
- ☐ Move snow shovels and snow blowers to a convenient spot.
- ☐ _____

☐ _____
☐ _____
☐ _____
☐ _____

Indoor Tasks:

☐ Change or clean furnace filters. Consult manufacturer instructions for your furnace to determine how frequently the filters should be replaced.
☐ Clean kitchen appliances inside and out, including refrigerator coils.
☐ Maintain clean drains by adding one-half-cup baking soda followed by one-half-cup white vinegar. After 10 minutes, flush with boiling water.
☐ _____
☐ _____
☐ _____
☐ _____
☐ _____

See Manufacturer's recommendations for product specific maintenance.

Year 2

Spring Home Maintenance

In spring, focus on freshening up your home and protecting your property against the season's strong winds and rains.

Outdoor Tasks:

- ☐ Clean gutters, downspouts, and drains.
- ☐ Inspect roof and chimney for cracks and damage. Inspect all sheet metal – caulk and repaint as needed.
- ☐ Clean deck, patio, porch surfaces, and inspect for surface damage or loose fasteners.
- ☐ Touch up peeling or damaged paint.
- ☐ Check for loose or missing address numbers, or numbers obscured by trees or vines. Clean, paint or polish as needed. Trim or prune any plants covering the numbers or blocking the view from the street. Check numbers at night to verify operation of installed lighting (if any).
- ☐ Lubricate and adjust garage door tracks, rollers, springs, drive chains, screw rods, hinges, door panels, etc. Inspect garage door for scratches or damage, repaint as necessary.
- ☐ Inspect and lubricate gate hinges, latches and locksets. Repaint as needed.
- ☐ Door Chime operates properly.
- ☐ Wash all windows, inside and out.
- ☐ Install screens on windows and doors.
- ☐ Clean outdoor furniture and air out cushions.
- ☐ Service your lawn mower.
- ☐ Irrigation is operational and adjusted to not spray the house.
- ☐ Fertilize your lawn.
- ☐ _____
- ☐ _____
- ☐ _____
- ☐ _____
- ☐ _____

Indoor Tasks:

- ☐ Test smoke and carbon monoxide detectors when you set clocks forward.
- ☐ If your basement has a sump pump, test it by dumping a large bucket of water into the basin of the sump pump. This should activate the sump pump. If it does not switch on or if it's not pumping water, it may need to be serviced by a professional. Also, check for and remove any debris and make sure there are no leaks.
- ☐ Wash and change seasonal bedding.
- ☐ Dust blinds and vacuum curtains throughout your house.
- ☐ Clean kitchen and bathroom cabinets and throw away outdated food, medicine and cosmetics.
- ☐ Inspect and re-caulk any area in kitchen and bathroom where dissimilar materials meet (bathtub-to-tile, toilet-to-floor, sink-to-countertop, etc.) and separation has occurred.
- ☐ Inspect all plumbing fixtures for leaks.
- ☐ Check all porcelain fixtures for cracks.
- ☐ _____
- ☐ _____
- ☐ _____
- ☐ _____
- ☐ _____

Summer Home Maintenance

In summer, complete the following projects to keep your yard lush and your home cool.

Outdoor Tasks:

- ☐ Walk around your home's exterior and slide open crawl space vents at the foundation.
- ☐ Prune trees and shrubs.
- ☐ Inspect and lubricate mailbox hinges, latches, and locks. Paint as needed.
- ☐ Inspect for pests and wood destroying organism activity.

- ☐ Remove lint from dryer exhaust vent with a long, flexible brush.
- ☐ Uncover central air conditioner and install window air conditioners.
- ☐ Inspect gas meter and pipes for rust and corrosion. Remove rust, prep and paint as necessary.
- ☐ _____
- ☐ _____
- ☐ _____
- ☐ _____
- ☐ _____

Indoor Tasks:

- ☐ Change or clean heating, ventilating and air conditioning filters. Consult manufacturer instructions for your furnace to determine whether you need to change filters more frequently. Learn more about choosing a filter.
- ☐ Clean kitchen appliances inside and out, including refrigerator coils.
- ☐ Maintain clean drains by adding a half-cup of baking soda followed by a half-cup of white vinegar. After 10 minutes, flush with boiling water.
- ☐ Drain or flush water heater.
- ☐ _____
- ☐ _____
- ☐ _____
- ☐ _____
- ☐ _____

Fall Home Maintenance

In fall, prepare your home and yard for cooler temperatures, falling leaves and more hours spent indoors.

Outdoor Tasks:

- ☐ Clean gutters and downspouts.
- ☐ Water flows freely away from house and does not pond excessively on patios, decks, porches, etc
- ☐ Inspect roof and chimney for cracks and damage.
- ☐ Inspect all attic block vents, roof vents and gable end vents to verify that the screens are intact ant that no debris is blocking the screens. Replace any missing or damaged screens.
- ☐ Check for loose or missing address numbers, or numbers obscured by trees or vines. Clean, paint or polish as needed. Trim or prune any plants covering the numbers or blocking the view from the street. Check numbers at night to verify operation of installed lighting (if any)
- ☐ Rake leaves and shred to use as mulch or dispose of them based on local guidelines.
- ☐ Close or install storm windows. Clean tracks and lubricate locking hardware, rollers, etc. Be sure weep holes in windows are clear, and free of debris (if applicable).
- ☐ Remove hoses from spigots and drain and store indoors, coiled and flat.
- ☐ Store outdoor furniture and cushions.
- ☐ Test snow blower and have it professionally serviced if necessary.
- ☐ Rake Leaves
- ☐ _____
- ☐ _____
- ☐ _____
- ☐ _____
- ☐ _____

Indoor Tasks:

- ☐ Test smoke and carbon monoxide detectors when you set clocks back in the fall.
- ☐ Check windows and doors for weather-tightness and install weather stripping where it's needed.
- ☐ Have furnace professionally inspected.
- ☐ If needed, set traps for rodents.
- ☐ Dust blinds and vacuum curtains throughout your house.
- ☐ Clean kitchen and bathroom cabinets and throw away outdated food, medicine and cosmetics.
- ☐ Inspect and re-caulk any area in kitchen and bathroom where dissimilar materials meet (bathtub-to-tile, toilet-to-floor, sink-to-countertop, countertop-to-backsplash, etc.) and separation has occurred.
- ☐ Inspect all plumbing fixtures for leaks.
- ☐ Check all porcelain fixtures for cracks.
- ☐ _____
- ☐ _____
- ☐ _____
- ☐ _____
- ☐ _____

Winter Home Maintenance

In winter, enjoy energy-efficient warmth and the fruits of your home-maintenance labors. Use this time of the year to thoroughly clean and care for your home's interior while taking a few precautionary measures on the outside.

Outdoor Tasks:

- ☐ Walk around your home's exterior and check the crawl space vents located at the foundation. Close any that are open.
- ☐ Protect your central air conditioning unit with a cover, and remove and store window air conditioners.
- ☐ Clean and store garden tools.
- ☐ Move snow shovels and snow blowers to a convenient spot.
- ☐ _____

- ☐ _____
- ☐ _____
- ☐ _____
- ☐ _____

Indoor Tasks:

- ☐ Change or clean furnace filters. Consult manufacturer instructions for your furnace to determine how frequently the filters should be replaced.
- ☐ Clean kitchen appliances inside and out, including refrigerator coils.
- ☐ Maintain clean drains by adding one-half-cup baking soda followed by one-half-cup white vinegar. After 10 minutes, flush with boiling water.
- ☐ _____
- ☐ _____
- ☐ _____
- ☐ _____
- ☐ _____

See Manufacturer's recommendations for product specific maintenance.

Year 3

Spring Home Maintenance

In spring, focus on freshening up your home and protecting your property against the season's strong winds and rains.

Outdoor Tasks:

- ☐ Clean gutters, downspouts, and drains.
- ☐ Inspect roof and chimney for cracks and damage. Inspect all sheet metal – caulk and repaint as needed.
- ☐ Clean deck, patio, porch surfaces, and inspect for surface damage or loose fasteners.
- ☐ Repaint wood surfaces.
- ☐ Check for loose or missing address numbers, or numbers obscured by trees or vines. Clean, paint or polish as needed. Trim or prune any plants covering the numbers or blocking the view from the street. Check numbers at night to verify operation of installed lighting (if any).
- ☐ Lubricate and adjust garage door tracks, rollers, springs, drive chains, screw rods, hinges, door panels, etc. Inspect garage door for scratches or damage, repaint as necessary.
- ☐ Inspect and lubricate gate hinges, latches and locksets. Repaint as needed.
- ☐ Door Chime operates properly.
- ☐ Wash all windows, inside and out.
- ☐ Install screens on windows and doors.
- ☐ Clean outdoor furniture and air out cushions.
- ☐ Service your lawn mower.
- ☐ Irrigation is operational and adjusted to not spray the house.
- ☐ Fertilize your lawn.
- ☐ _____
- ☐ _____
- ☐ _____
- ☐ _____
- ☐ _____

Indoor Tasks:

- ☐ Test smoke and carbon monoxide detectors when you set clocks forward.
- ☐ If your basement has a sump pump, test it by dumping a large bucket of water into the basin of the sump pump. This should activate the sump pump. If it does not switch on or if it's not pumping water, it may need to be serviced by a professional. Also, check for and remove any debris and make sure there are no leaks.
- ☐ Wash and change seasonal bedding.
- ☐ Dust blinds and vacuum curtains throughout your house.
- ☐ Clean kitchen and bathroom cabinets and throw away outdated food, medicine and cosmetics.
- ☐ Inspect and re-caulk any area in kitchen and bathroom where dissimilar materials meet (bathtub-to-tile, toilet-to-floor, sink-to-countertop, etc.) and separation has occurred.
- ☐ Inspect all plumbing fixtures for leaks.
- ☐ Check all porcelain fixtures for cracks.
- ☐ _____
- ☐ _____
- ☐ _____
- ☐ _____
- ☐ _____

Summer Home Maintenance

In summer, complete the following projects to keep your yard lush and your home cool.

Outdoor Tasks:

- ☐ Walk around your home's exterior and slide open crawl space vents at the foundation.
- ☐ Prune trees and shrubs.
- ☐ Inspect and lubricate mailbox hinges, latches, and locks. Paint as needed.
- ☐ Inspect for pests and wood destroying organism activity.

- ☐ Remove lint from dryer exhaust vent with a long, flexible brush.
- ☐ Uncover central air conditioner and install window air conditioners.
- ☐ Inspect gas meter and pipes for rust and corrosion. Remove rust, prep and paint as necessary.
- ☐ _____
- ☐ _____
- ☐ _____
- ☐ _____
- ☐ _____

Indoor Tasks:

- ☐ Change or clean heating, ventilating and air conditioning filters. Consult manufacturer instructions for your furnace to determine whether you need to change filters more frequently. Learn more about choosing a filter.
- ☐ Clean kitchen appliances inside and out, including refrigerator coils.
- ☐ Maintain clean drains by adding a half-cup of baking soda followed by a half-cup of white vinegar. After 10 minutes, flush with boiling water.
- ☐ Drain or flush water heater.
- ☐ _____
- ☐ _____
- ☐ _____
- ☐ _____
- ☐ _____

Fall Home Maintenance

In fall, prepare your home and yard for cooler temperatures, falling leaves and more hours spent indoors.

Outdoor Tasks:

- ☐ Clean gutters and downspouts.
- ☐ Water flows freely away from house and does not pond excessively on patios, decks, porches, etc.
- ☐ Inspect roof and chimney for cracks and damage.
- ☐ Inspect all attic block vents, roof vents and gable end vents to verify that the screens are intact ant that no debris is blocking the screens. Replace any missing or damaged screens.
- ☐ Check for loose or missing address numbers, or numbers obscured by trees or vines. Clean, paint or polish as needed. Trim or prune any plants covering the numbers or blocking the view from the street. Check numbers at night to verify operation of installed lighting (if any)
- ☐ Rake leaves and shred to use as mulch or dispose of them based on local guidelines.
- ☐ Close or install storm windows. Clean tracks and lubricate locking hardware, rollers, etc. Be sure weep holes in windows are clear, and free of debris (if applicable).
- ☐ Remove hoses from spigots and drain and store indoors, coiled and flat.
- ☐ Store outdoor furniture and cushions.
- ☐ Test snow blower and have it professionally serviced if necessary.
- ☐ Rake Leaves
- ☐ _____
- ☐ _____
- ☐ _____
- ☐ _____
- ☐ _____

Indoor Tasks:

- ☐ Test smoke and carbon monoxide detectors when you set clocks back in the fall.
- ☐ Check windows and doors for weather-tightness and install weather stripping where it's needed.
- ☐ Have furnace professionally inspected.
- ☐ If needed, set traps for rodents.
- ☐ Dust blinds and vacuum curtains throughout your house.
- ☐ Clean kitchen and bathroom cabinets and throw away outdated food, medicine and cosmetics.
- ☐ Inspect and re-caulk any area in kitchen and bathroom where dissimilar materials meet (bathtub-to-tile, toilet-to-floor, sink-to-countertop, countertop-to-backsplash, etc.) and separation has occurred.
- ☐ Inspect all plumbing fixtures for leaks.
- ☐ Check all porcelain fixtures for cracks.
- ☐ _____
- ☐ _____
- ☐ _____
- ☐ _____
- ☐ _____

Winter Home Maintenance

In winter, enjoy energy-efficient warmth and the fruits of your home-maintenance labors. Use this time of the year to thoroughly clean and care for your home's interior while taking a few precautionary measures on the outside.

Outdoor Tasks:

- ☐ Walk around your home's exterior and check the crawl space vents located at the foundation. Close any that are open.
- ☐ Protect your central air conditioning unit with a cover, and remove and store window air conditioners.
- ☐ Clean and store garden tools.
- ☐ Move snow shovels and snow blowers to a convenient spot.
- ☐ _____

☐ _____
☐ _____
☐ _____
☐ _____

Indoor Tasks:

☐ Change or clean furnace filters. Consult manufacturer instructions for your furnace to determine how frequently the filters should be replaced.
☐ Clean kitchen appliances inside and out, including refrigerator coils.
☐ Maintain clean drains by adding one-half-cup baking soda followed by one-half-cup white vinegar. After 10 minutes, flush with boiling water.
☐ _____
☐ _____
☐ _____
☐ _____
☐ _____

See Manufacturer's recommendations for product specific maintenance

Year 4

Spring Home Maintenance

In spring, focus on freshening up your home and protecting your property against the season's strong winds and rains.

Outdoor Tasks:

- ☐ Clean gutters, downspouts, and drains.
- ☐ Inspect roof and chimney for cracks and damage. Inspect all sheet metal – caulk and repaint as needed.
- ☐ Clean deck, patio, porch surfaces, and inspect for surface damage or loose fasteners.
- ☐ Touch up peeling or damaged paint.
- ☐ Check for loose or missing address numbers, or numbers obscured by trees or vines. Clean, paint or polish as needed. Trim or prune any plants covering the numbers or blocking the view from the street. Check numbers at night to verify operation of installed lighting (if any).
- ☐ Lubricate and adjust garage door tracks, rollers, springs, drive chains, screw rods, hinges, door panels, etc. Inspect garage door for scratches or damage, repaint as necessary.
- ☐ Inspect and lubricate gate hinges, latches and locksets. Repaint as needed.
- ☐ Door Chime operates properly.
- ☐ Wash all windows, inside and out.
- ☐ Install screens on windows and doors.
- ☐ Clean outdoor furniture and air out cushions.
- ☐ Service your lawn mower.
- ☐ Irrigation is operational and adjusted to not spray the house.
- ☐ Fertilize your lawn.
- ☐ _____
- ☐ _____
- ☐ _____
- ☐ _____
- ☐ _____

Indoor Tasks:

- ☐ Test smoke and carbon monoxide detectors when you set clocks forward.
- ☐ If your basement has a sump pump, test it by dumping a large bucket of water into the basin of the sump pump. This should activate the sump pump. If it does not switch on or if it's not pumping water, it may need to be serviced by a professional. Also, check for and remove any debris and make sure there are no leaks.
- ☐ Wash and change seasonal bedding.
- ☐ Dust blinds and vacuum curtains throughout your house.
- ☐ Clean kitchen and bathroom cabinets and throw away outdated food, medicine and cosmetics.
- ☐ Inspect and re-caulk any area in kitchen and bathroom where dissimilar materials meet (bathtub-to-tile, toilet-to-floor, sink-to-countertop, etc.) and separation has occurred.
- ☐ Inspect all plumbing fixtures for leaks.
- ☐ Check all porcelain fixtures for cracks.
- ☐ _____
- ☐ _____
- ☐ _____
- ☐ _____
- ☐ _____

Summer Home Maintenance

In summer, complete the following projects to keep your yard lush and your home cool.

Outdoor Tasks:

- ☐ Walk around your home's exterior and slide open crawl space vents at the foundation.
- ☐ Prune trees and shrubs.
- ☐ Inspect and lubricate mailbox hinges, latches, and locks. Paint as needed.
- ☐ Inspect for pests and wood destroying organism activity.

- ☐ Remove lint from dryer exhaust vent with a long, flexible brush.
- ☐ Uncover central air conditioner and install window air conditioners.
- ☐ Inspect gas meter and pipes for rust and corrosion. Remove rust, prep and paint as necessary.
- ☐ _____
- ☐ _____
- ☐ _____
- ☐ _____
- ☐ _____

Indoor Tasks:

- ☐ Change or clean heating, ventilating and air conditioning filters. Consult manufacturer instructions for your furnace to determine whether you need to change filters more frequently. Learn more about choosing a filter.
- ☐ Clean kitchen appliances inside and out, including refrigerator coils.
- ☐ Maintain clean drains by adding a half-cup of baking soda followed by a half-cup of white vinegar. After 10 minutes, flush with boiling water.
- ☐ Drain or flush water heater.
- ☐ _____
- ☐ _____
- ☐ _____
- ☐ _____
- ☐ _____

Fall Home Maintenance

In fall, prepare your home and yard for cooler temperatures, falling leaves and more hours spent indoors.

Outdoor Tasks:

- ☐ Clean gutters and downspouts.
- ☐ Water flows freely away from house and does not pond excessively on patios, decks, porches, etc
- ☐ Inspect roof and chimney for cracks and damage.
- ☐ Inspect all attic block vents, roof vents and gable end vents to verify that the screens are intact ant that no debris is blocking the screens. Replace any missing or damaged screens.
- ☐ Check for loose or missing address numbers, or numbers obscured by trees or vines. Clean, paint or polish as needed. Trim or prune any plants covering the numbers or blocking the view from the street. Check numbers at night to verify operation of installed lighting (if any)
- ☐ Rake leaves and shred to use as mulch or dispose of them based on local guidelines.
- ☐ Close or install storm windows. Clean tracks and lubricate locking hardware, rollers, etc. Be sure weep holes in windows are clear, and free of debris (if applicable).
- ☐ Remove hoses from spigots and drain and store indoors, coiled and flat.
- ☐ Store outdoor furniture and cushions.
- ☐ Test snow blower and have it professionally serviced if necessary.
- ☐ Rake Leaves
- ☐ _____
- ☐ _____
- ☐ _____
- ☐ _____
- ☐ _____

Indoor Tasks:

- ☐ Test smoke and carbon monoxide detectors when you set clocks back in the fall.
- ☐ Check windows and doors for weather-tightness and install weather stripping where it's needed.
- ☐ Have furnace professionally inspected.
- ☐ If needed, set traps for rodents.
- ☐ Dust blinds and vacuum curtains throughout your house.
- ☐ Clean kitchen and bathroom cabinets and throw away outdated food, medicine and cosmetics.
- ☐ Inspect and re-caulk any area in kitchen and bathroom where dissimilar materials meet (bathtub-to-tile, toilet-to-floor, sink-to-countertop, countertop-to-backsplash, etc.) and separation has occurred.
- ☐ Inspect all plumbing fixtures for leaks.
- ☐ Check all porcelain fixtures for cracks.
- ☐ _____
- ☐ _____
- ☐ _____
- ☐ _____
- ☐ _____

Winter Home Maintenance

In winter, enjoy energy-efficient warmth and the fruits of your home-maintenance labors. Use this time of the year to thoroughly clean and care for your home's interior while taking a few precautionary measures on the outside.

Outdoor Tasks:

- ☐ Walk around your home's exterior and check the crawl space vents located at the foundation. Close any that are open.
- ☐ Protect your central air conditioning unit with a cover, and remove and store window air conditioners.
- ☐ Clean and store garden tools.
- ☐ Move snow shovels and snow blowers to a convenient spot.
- ☐ _____

☐ _____
☐ _____
☐ _____
☐ _____

Indoor Tasks:

☐ Change or clean furnace filters. Consult manufacturer instructions for your furnace to determine how frequently the filters should be replaced.
☐ Clean kitchen appliances inside and out, including refrigerator coils.
☐ Maintain clean drains by adding one-half-cup baking soda followed by one-half-cup white vinegar. After 10 minutes, flush with boiling water.
☐ _____
☐ _____
☐ _____
☐ _____
☐ _____

See Manufacturer's recommendations for product specific maintenance

Year 5

Spring Home Maintenance

In spring, focus on freshening up your home and protecting your property against the season's strong winds and rains.

Outdoor Tasks:

- ☐ Clean gutters, downspouts, and drains.
- ☐ Inspect roof and chimney for cracks and damage. Inspect all sheet metal – caulk and repaint as needed.
- ☐ Clean deck, patio, porch surfaces, and inspect for surface damage or loose fasteners.
- ☐ Touch up peeling or damaged paint.
- ☐ Check for loose or missing address numbers, or numbers obscured by trees or vines. Clean, paint or polish as needed. Trim or prune any plants covering the numbers or blocking the view from the street. Check numbers at night to verify operation of installed lighting (if any).
- ☐ Lubricate and adjust garage door tracks, rollers, springs, drive chains, screw rods, hinges, door panels, etc. Inspect garage door for scratches or damage, repaint as necessary.
- ☐ Inspect and lubricate gate hinges, latches and locksets. Repaint as needed.
- ☐ Door Chime operates properly.
- ☐ Wash all windows, inside and out.
- ☐ Install screens on windows and doors.
- ☐ Clean outdoor furniture and air out cushions.
- ☐ Service your lawn mower.
- ☐ Irrigation is operational and adjusted to not spray the house.
- ☐ Fertilize your lawn.
- ☐ _____
- ☐ _____
- ☐ _____
- ☐ _____
- ☐ _____

Indoor Tasks:

- ☐ Test smoke and carbon monoxide detectors when you set clocks forward.
- ☐ If your basement has a sump pump, test it by dumping a large bucket of water into the basin of the sump pump. This should activate the sump pump. If it does not switch on or if it's not pumping water, it may need to be serviced by a professional. Also, check for and remove any debris and make sure there are no leaks.
- ☐ Wash and change seasonal bedding.
- ☐ Dust blinds and vacuum curtains throughout your house.
- ☐ Clean kitchen and bathroom cabinets and throw away outdated food, medicine and cosmetics.
- ☐ Inspect and re-caulk any area in kitchen and bathroom where dissimilar materials meet (bathtub-to-tile, toilet-to-floor, sink-to-countertop, etc.) and separation has occurred.
- ☐ Inspect all plumbing fixtures for leaks.
- ☐ Check all porcelain fixtures for cracks.
- ☐ _____
- ☐ _____
- ☐ _____
- ☐ _____
- ☐ _____

Summer Home Maintenance

In summer, complete the following projects to keep your yard lush and your home cool.

Outdoor Tasks:

- ☐ Walk around your home's exterior and slide open crawl space vents at the foundation.
- ☐ Prune trees and shrubs.
- ☐ Inspect and lubricate mailbox hinges, latches, and locks. Paint as needed.
- ☐ Inspect for pests and wood destroying organism activity.

- ☐ Remove lint from dryer exhaust vent with a long, flexible brush.
- ☐ Uncover central air conditioner and install window air conditioners.
- ☐ Inspect gas meter and pipes for rust and corrosion. Remove rust, prep and paint as necessary.
- ☐ _____
- ☐ _____
- ☐ _____
- ☐ _____
- ☐ _____

Indoor Tasks:

- ☐ Change or clean heating, ventilating and air conditioning filters. Consult manufacturer instructions for your furnace to determine whether you need to change filters more frequently. Learn more about choosing a filter.
- ☐ Clean kitchen appliances inside and out, including refrigerator coils.
- ☐ Maintain clean drains by adding a half-cup of baking soda followed by a half-cup of white vinegar. After 10 minutes, flush with boiling water.
- ☐ Drain or flush water heater.
- ☐ _____
- ☐ _____
- ☐ _____
- ☐ _____
- ☐ _____

Fall Home Maintenance

In fall, prepare your home and yard for cooler temperatures, falling leaves and more hours spent indoors.

Outdoor Tasks:

- ☐ Clean gutters and downspouts.
- ☐ Water flows freely away from house and does not pond excessively on patios, decks, porches, etc
- ☐ Inspect roof and chimney for cracks and damage.
- ☐ Inspect all attic block vents, roof vents and gable end vents to verify that the screens are intact ant that no debris is blocking the screens. Replace any missing or damaged screens.
- ☐ Check for loose or missing address numbers, or numbers obscured by trees or vines. Clean, paint or polish as needed. Trim or prune any plants covering the numbers or blocking the view from the street. Check numbers at night to verify operation of installed lighting (if any)
- ☐ Rake leaves and shred to use as mulch or dispose of them based on local guidelines.
- ☐ Close or install storm windows. Clean tracks and lubricate locking hardware, rollers, etc. Be sure weep holes in windows are clear, and free of debris (if applicable).
- ☐ Remove hoses from spigots and drain and store indoors, coiled and flat.
- ☐ Store outdoor furniture and cushions.
- ☐ Test snow blower and have it professionally serviced if necessary.
- ☐ Rake Leaves
- ☐ _____
- ☐ _____
- ☐ _____
- ☐ _____
- ☐ _____

Indoor Tasks:

- ☐ Test smoke and carbon monoxide detectors when you set clocks back in the fall.
- ☐ Check windows and doors for weather-tightness and install weather stripping where it's needed.
- ☐ Have furnace professionally inspected.
- ☐ If needed, set traps for rodents.
- ☐ Dust blinds and vacuum curtains throughout your house.
- ☐ Clean kitchen and bathroom cabinets and throw away outdated food, medicine and cosmetics.
- ☐ Inspect and re-caulk any area in kitchen and bathroom where dissimilar materials meet (bathtub-to-tile, toilet-to-floor, sink-to-countertop, countertop-to-backsplash, etc.) and separation has occurred.
- ☐ Inspect all plumbing fixtures for leaks.
- ☐ Check all porcelain fixtures for cracks.
- ☐ _____
- ☐ _____
- ☐ _____
- ☐ _____
- ☐ _____

Winter Home Maintenance

In winter, enjoy energy-efficient warmth and the fruits of your home-maintenance labors. Use this time of the year to thoroughly clean and care for your home's interior while taking a few precautionary measures on the outside.

Outdoor Tasks:

- ☐ Walk around your home's exterior and check the crawl space vents located at the foundation. Close any that are open.
- ☐ Protect your central air conditioning unit with a cover, and remove and store window air conditioners.
- ☐ Clean and store garden tools.
- ☐ Move snow shovels and snow blowers to a convenient spot.
- ☐ _____

☐ _____
☐ _____
☐ _____
☐ _____

Indoor Tasks:

☐ Change or clean furnace filters. Consult manufacturer instructions for your furnace to determine how frequently the filters should be replaced.
☐ Clean kitchen appliances inside and out, including refrigerator coils.
☐ Maintain clean drains by adding one-half-cup baking soda followed by one-half-cup white vinegar. After 10 minutes, flush with boiling water.
☐ _____
☐ _____
☐ _____
☐ _____
☐ _____

See Manufacturer's recommendations for product specific maintenance

Year 6

Spring Home Maintenance

In spring, focus on freshening up your home and protecting your property against the season's strong winds and rains.

Outdoor Tasks:

- ☐ Clean gutters, downspouts, and drains.
- ☐ Inspect roof and chimney for cracks and damage. Inspect all sheet metal – caulk and repaint as needed.
- ☐ Clean deck, patio, porch surfaces, and inspect for surface damage or loose fasteners.
- ☐ Repaint wood surfaces.
- ☐ Check for loose or missing address numbers, or numbers obscured by trees or vines. Clean, paint or polish as needed. Trim or prune any plants covering the numbers or blocking the view from the street. Check numbers at night to verify operation of installed lighting (if any).
- ☐ Lubricate and adjust garage door tracks, rollers, springs, drive chains, screw rods, hinges, door panels, etc. Inspect garage door for scratches or damage, repaint as necessary.
- ☐ Inspect and lubricate gate hinges, latches and locksets. Repaint as needed.
- ☐ Door Chime operates properly.
- ☐ Wash all windows, inside and out.
- ☐ Install screens on windows and doors.
- ☐ Clean outdoor furniture and air out cushions.
- ☐ Service your lawn mower.
- ☐ Irrigation is operational and adjusted to not spray the house.
- ☐ Fertilize your lawn.
- ☐ _____
- ☐ _____
- ☐ _____
- ☐ _____
- ☐ _____

Indoor Tasks:

- ☐ Test smoke and carbon monoxide detectors when you set clocks forward.
- ☐ If your basement has a sump pump, test it by dumping a large bucket of water into the basin of the sump pump. This should activate the sump pump. If it does not switch on or if it's not pumping water, it may need to be serviced by a professional. Also, check for and remove any debris and make sure there are no leaks.
- ☐ Wash and change seasonal bedding.
- ☐ Dust blinds and vacuum curtains throughout your house.
- ☐ Clean kitchen and bathroom cabinets and throw away outdated food, medicine and cosmetics.
- ☐ Inspect and re-caulk any area in kitchen and bathroom where dissimilar materials meet (bathtub-to-tile, toilet-to-floor, sink-to-countertop, etc.) and separation has occurred.
- ☐ Inspect all plumbing fixtures for leaks.
- ☐ Check all porcelain fixtures for cracks.
- ☐ _____
- ☐ _____
- ☐ _____
- ☐ _____
- ☐ _____

Summer Home Maintenance

In summer, complete the following projects to keep your yard lush and your home cool.

Outdoor Tasks:

- ☐ Walk around your home's exterior and slide open crawl space vents at the foundation.
- ☐ Prune trees and shrubs.
- ☐ Inspect and lubricate mailbox hinges, latches, and locks. Paint as needed.
- ☐ Inspect for pests and wood destroying organism activity.

- ☐ Remove lint from dryer exhaust vent with a long, flexible brush.
- ☐ Uncover central air conditioner and install window air conditioners.
- ☐ Inspect gas meter and pipes for rust and corrosion. Remove rust, prep and paint as necessary.
- ☐ _____
- ☐ _____
- ☐ _____
- ☐ _____
- ☐ _____

Indoor Tasks:

- ☐ Change or clean heating, ventilating and air conditioning filters. Consult manufacturer instructions for your furnace to determine whether you need to change filters more frequently. Learn more about choosing a filter.
- ☐ Clean kitchen appliances inside and out, including refrigerator coils.
- ☐ Maintain clean drains by adding a half-cup of baking soda followed by a half-cup of white vinegar. After 10 minutes, flush with boiling water.
- ☐ Drain or flush water heater.
- ☐ _____
- ☐ _____
- ☐ _____
- ☐ _____
- ☐ _____

Fall Home Maintenance

In fall, prepare your home and yard for cooler temperatures, falling leaves and more hours spent indoors.

Outdoor Tasks:

- ☐ Clean gutters and downspouts.
- ☐ Water flows freely away from house and does not pond excessively on patios, decks, porches, etc.
- ☐ Inspect roof and chimney for cracks and damage.
- ☐ Inspect all attic block vents, roof vents and gable end vents to verify that the screens are intact ant that no debris is blocking the screens. Replace any missing or damaged screens.
- ☐ Check for loose or missing address numbers, or numbers obscured by trees or vines. Clean, paint or polish as needed. Trim or prune any plants covering the numbers or blocking the view from the street. Check numbers at night to verify operation of installed lighting (if any)
- ☐ Rake leaves and shred to use as mulch or dispose of them based on local guidelines.
- ☐ Close or install storm windows. Clean tracks and lubricate locking hardware, rollers, etc. Be sure weep holes in windows are clear, and free of debris (if applicable).
- ☐ Remove hoses from spigots and drain and store indoors, coiled and flat.
- ☐ Store outdoor furniture and cushions.
- ☐ Test snow blower and have it professionally serviced if necessary.
- ☐ Rake Leaves
- ☐ _____
- ☐ _____
- ☐ _____
- ☐ _____
- ☐ _____

Indoor Tasks:

- ☐ Test smoke and carbon monoxide detectors when you set clocks back in the fall.
- ☐ Check windows and doors for weather-tightness and install weather stripping where it's needed.
- ☐ Have furnace professionally inspected.
- ☐ If needed, set traps for rodents.
- ☐ Dust blinds and vacuum curtains throughout your house.
- ☐ Clean kitchen and bathroom cabinets and throw away outdated food, medicine and cosmetics.
- ☐ Inspect and re-caulk any area in kitchen and bathroom where dissimilar materials meet (bathtub-to-tile, toilet-to-floor, sink-to-countertop, countertop-to-backsplash, etc.) and separation has occurred.
- ☐ Inspect all plumbing fixtures for leaks.
- ☐ Check all porcelain fixtures for cracks.
- ☐ _____
- ☐ _____
- ☐ _____
- ☐ _____
- ☐ _____

Winter Home Maintenance

In winter, enjoy energy-efficient warmth and the fruits of your home-maintenance labors. Use this time of the year to thoroughly clean and care for your home's interior while taking a few precautionary measures on the outside.

Outdoor Tasks:

- ☐ Walk around your home's exterior and check the crawl space vents located at the foundation. Close any that are open.
- ☐ Protect your central air conditioning unit with a cover, and remove and store window air conditioners.
- ☐ Clean and store garden tools.
- ☐ Move snow shovels and snow blowers to a convenient spot.
- ☐ _____

- ☐ _____
- ☐ _____
- ☐ _____
- ☐ _____

Indoor Tasks:

- ☐ Change or clean furnace filters. Consult manufacturer instructions for your furnace to determine how frequently the filters should be replaced.
- ☐ Clean kitchen appliances inside and out, including refrigerator coils.
- ☐ Maintain clean drains by adding one-half-cup baking soda followed by one-half-cup white vinegar. After 10 minutes, flush with boiling water.
- ☐ _____
- ☐ _____
- ☐ _____
- ☐ _____
- ☐ _____

See Manufacturer's recommendations for product specific maintenance

Year 7

Spring Home Maintenance

In spring, focus on freshening up your home and protecting your property against the season's strong winds and rains.

Outdoor Tasks:

- ☐ Clean gutters, downspouts, and drains.
- ☐ Inspect roof and chimney for cracks and damage. Inspect all sheet metal – caulk and repaint as needed.
- ☐ Clean deck, patio, porch surfaces, and inspect for surface damage or loose fasteners.
- ☐ Touch up peeling or damaged paint.
- ☐ Check for loose or missing address numbers, or numbers obscured by trees or vines. Clean, paint or polish as needed. Trim or prune any plants covering the numbers or blocking the view from the street. Check numbers at night to verify operation of installed lighting (if any).
- ☐ Lubricate and adjust garage door tracks, rollers, springs, drive chains, screw rods, hinges, door panels, etc. Inspect garage door for scratches or damage, repaint as necessary.
- ☐ Inspect and lubricate gate hinges, latches and locksets. Repaint as needed.
- ☐ Door Chime operates properly.
- ☐ Wash all windows, inside and out.
- ☐ Install screens on windows and doors.
- ☐ Clean outdoor furniture and air out cushions.
- ☐ Service your lawn mower.
- ☐ Irrigation is operational and adjusted to not spray the house.
- ☐ Fertilize your lawn.
- ☐ _____
- ☐ _____
- ☐ _____
- ☐ _____
- ☐ _____

Indoor Tasks:

- ☐ Test smoke and carbon monoxide detectors when you set clocks forward.
- ☐ If your basement has a sump pump, test it by dumping a large bucket of water into the basin of the sump pump. This should activate the sump pump. If it does not switch on or if it's not pumping water, it may need to be serviced by a professional. Also, check for and remove any debris and make sure there are no leaks.
- ☐ Wash and change seasonal bedding.
- ☐ Dust blinds and vacuum curtains throughout your house.
- ☐ Clean kitchen and bathroom cabinets and throw away outdated food, medicine and cosmetics.
- ☐ Inspect and re-caulk any area in kitchen and bathroom where dissimilar materials meet (bathtub-to-tile, toilet-to-floor, sink-to-countertop, etc.) and separation has occurred.
- ☐ Inspect all plumbing fixtures for leaks.
- ☐ Check all porcelain fixtures for cracks.
- ☐ _____
- ☐ _____
- ☐ _____
- ☐ _____
- ☐ _____

Summer Home Maintenance

In summer, complete the following projects to keep your yard lush and your home cool.

Outdoor Tasks:

- ☐ Walk around your home's exterior and slide open crawl space vents at the foundation.
- ☐ Prune trees and shrubs.
- ☐ Inspect and lubricate mailbox hinges, latches, and locks. Paint as needed.
- ☐ Inspect for pests and wood destroying organism activity.

- ☐ Remove lint from dryer exhaust vent with a long, flexible brush.
- ☐ Uncover central air conditioner and install window air conditioners.
- ☐ Inspect gas meter and pipes for rust and corrosion. Remove rust, prep and paint as necessary.
- ☐ _____
- ☐ _____
- ☐ _____
- ☐ _____
- ☐ _____

Indoor Tasks:

- ☐ Change or clean heating, ventilating and air conditioning filters. Consult manufacturer instructions for your furnace to determine whether you need to change filters more frequently. Learn more about choosing a filter.
- ☐ Clean kitchen appliances inside and out, including refrigerator coils.
- ☐ Maintain clean drains by adding a half-cup of baking soda followed by a half-cup of white vinegar. After 10 minutes, flush with boiling water.
- ☐ Drain or flush water heater.
- ☐ _____
- ☐ _____
- ☐ _____
- ☐ _____
- ☐ _____

Fall Home Maintenance

In fall, prepare your home and yard for cooler temperatures, falling leaves and more hours spent indoors.

Outdoor Tasks:

- ☐ Clean gutters and downspouts.
- ☐ Water flows freely away from house and does not pond excessively on patios, decks, porches, etc
- ☐ Inspect roof and chimney for cracks and damage.
- ☐ Inspect all attic block vents, roof vents and gable end vents to verify that the screens are intact ant that no debris is blocking the screens. Replace any missing or damaged screens.
- ☐ Check for loose or missing address numbers, or numbers obscured by trees or vines. Clean, paint or polish as needed. Trim or prune any plants covering the numbers or blocking the view from the street. Check numbers at night to verify operation of installed lighting (if any)
- ☐ Rake leaves and shred to use as mulch or dispose of them based on local guidelines.
- ☐ Close or install storm windows. Clean tracks and lubricate locking hardware, rollers, etc. Be sure weep holes in windows are clear, and free of debris (if applicable).
- ☐ Remove hoses from spigots and drain and store indoors, coiled and flat.
- ☐ Store outdoor furniture and cushions.
- ☐ Test snow blower and have it professionally serviced if necessary.
- ☐ Rake Leaves
- ☐ _____
- ☐ _____
- ☐ _____
- ☐ _____
- ☐ _____

Indoor Tasks:

- ☐ Test smoke and carbon monoxide detectors when you set clocks back in the fall.
- ☐ Check windows and doors for weather-tightness and install weather stripping where it's needed.
- ☐ Have furnace professionally inspected.
- ☐ If needed, set traps for rodents.
- ☐ Dust blinds and vacuum curtains throughout your house.
- ☐ Clean kitchen and bathroom cabinets and throw away outdated food, medicine and cosmetics.
- ☐ Inspect and re-caulk any area in kitchen and bathroom where dissimilar materials meet (bathtub-to-tile, toilet-to-floor, sink-to-countertop, countertop-to-backsplash, etc.) and separation has occurred.
- ☐ Inspect all plumbing fixtures for leaks.
- ☐ Check all porcelain fixtures for cracks.
- ☐ _____
- ☐ _____
- ☐ _____
- ☐ _____
- ☐ _____

Winter Home Maintenance

In winter, enjoy energy-efficient warmth and the fruits of your home-maintenance labors. Use this time of the year to thoroughly clean and care for your home's interior while taking a few precautionary measures on the outside.

Outdoor Tasks:

- ☐ Walk around your home's exterior and check the crawl space vents located at the foundation. Close any that are open.
- ☐ Protect your central air conditioning unit with a cover, and remove and store window air conditioners.
- ☐ Clean and store garden tools.
- ☐ Move snow shovels and snow blowers to a convenient spot.
- ☐ _____

☐ _____
☐ _____
☐ _____
☐ _____

Indoor Tasks:

☐ Change or clean furnace filters. Consult manufacturer instructions for your furnace to determine how frequently the filters should be replaced.
☐ Clean kitchen appliances inside and out, including refrigerator coils.
☐ Maintain clean drains by adding one-half-cup baking soda followed by one-half-cup white vinegar. After 10 minutes, flush with boiling water.
☐ _____
☐ _____
☐ _____
☐ _____
☐ _____

See Manufacturer's recommendations for product specific maintenance

Year 8

Spring Home Maintenance

In spring, focus on freshening up your home and protecting your property against the season's strong winds and rains.

Outdoor Tasks:

- ☐ Clean gutters, downspouts, and drains.
- ☐ Inspect roof and chimney for cracks and damage. Inspect all sheet metal – caulk and repaint as needed.
- ☐ Clean deck, patio, porch surfaces, and inspect for surface damage or loose fasteners.
- ☐ Touch up peeling or damaged paint.
- ☐ Check for loose or missing address numbers, or numbers obscured by trees or vines. Clean, paint or polish as needed. Trim or prune any plants covering the numbers or blocking the view from the street. Check numbers at night to verify operation of installed lighting (if any).
- ☐ Lubricate and adjust garage door tracks, rollers, springs, drive chains, screw rods, hinges, door panels, etc. Inspect garage door for scratches or damage, repaint as necessary.
- ☐ Inspect and lubricate gate hinges, latches and locksets. Repaint as needed.
- ☐ Door Chime operates properly.
- ☐ Wash all windows, inside and out.
- ☐ Install screens on windows and doors.
- ☐ Clean outdoor furniture and air out cushions.
- ☐ Service your lawn mower.
- ☐ Irrigation is operational and adjusted to not spray the house.
- ☐ Fertilize your lawn.
- ☐ _____
- ☐ _____
- ☐ _____
- ☐ _____
- ☐ _____

Indoor Tasks:

- [ ] Test smoke and carbon monoxide detectors when you set clocks forward.
- [ ] If your basement has a sump pump, test it by dumping a large bucket of water into the basin of the sump pump. This should activate the sump pump. If it does not switch on or if it's not pumping water, it may need to be serviced by a professional. Also, check for and remove any debris and make sure there are no leaks.
- [ ] Wash and change seasonal bedding.
- [ ] Dust blinds and vacuum curtains throughout your house.
- [ ] Clean kitchen and bathroom cabinets and throw away outdated food, medicine and cosmetics.
- [ ] Inspect and re-caulk any area in kitchen and bathroom where dissimilar materials meet (bathtub-to-tile, toilet-to-floor, sink-to-countertop, etc.) and separation has occurred.
- [ ] Inspect all plumbing fixtures for leaks.
- [ ] Check all porcelain fixtures for cracks.
- [ ] _____
- [ ] _____
- [ ] _____
- [ ] _____
- [ ] _____

Summer Home Maintenance

In summer, complete the following projects to keep your yard lush and your home cool.

Outdoor Tasks:

- [ ] Walk around your home's exterior and slide open crawl space vents at the foundation.
- [ ] Prune trees and shrubs.
- [ ] Inspect and lubricate mailbox hinges, latches, and locks. Paint as needed.
- [ ] Inspect for pests and wood destroying organism activity.

- ☐ Remove lint from dryer exhaust vent with a long, flexible brush.
- ☐ Uncover central air conditioner and install window air conditioners.
- ☐ Inspect gas meter and pipes for rust and corrosion. Remove rust, prep and paint as necessary.
- ☐ _____
- ☐ _____
- ☐ _____
- ☐ _____
- ☐ _____

Indoor Tasks:

- ☐ Change or clean heating, ventilating and air conditioning filters. Consult manufacturer instructions for your furnace to determine whether you need to change filters more frequently. Learn more about choosing a filter.
- ☐ Clean kitchen appliances inside and out, including refrigerator coils.
- ☐ Maintain clean drains by adding a half-cup of baking soda followed by a half-cup of white vinegar. After 10 minutes, flush with boiling water.
- ☐ Drain or flush water heater.
- ☐ _____
- ☐ _____
- ☐ _____
- ☐ _____
- ☐ _____

Fall Home Maintenance

In fall, prepare your home and yard for cooler temperatures, falling leaves and more hours spent indoors.

Outdoor Tasks:

- ☐ Clean gutters and downspouts.
- ☐ Water flows freely away from house and does not pond excessively on patios, decks, porches, etc
- ☐ Inspect roof and chimney for cracks and damage.
- ☐ Inspect all attic block vents, roof vents and gable end vents to verify that the screens are intact ant that no debris is blocking the screens. Replace any missing or damaged screens.
- ☐ Check for loose or missing address numbers, or numbers obscured by trees or vines. Clean, paint or polish as needed. Trim or prune any plants covering the numbers or blocking the view from the street. Check numbers at night to verify operation of installed lighting (if any)
- ☐ Rake leaves and shred to use as mulch or dispose of them based on local guidelines.
- ☐ Close or install storm windows. Clean tracks and lubricate locking hardware, rollers, etc. Be sure weep holes in windows are clear, and free of debris (if applicable).
- ☐ Remove hoses from spigots and drain and store indoors, coiled and flat.
- ☐ Store outdoor furniture and cushions.
- ☐ Test snow blower and have it professionally serviced if necessary.
- ☐ Rake Leaves
- ☐ _____
- ☐ _____
- ☐ _____
- ☐ _____
- ☐ _____

Indoor Tasks:

- ☐ Test smoke and carbon monoxide detectors when you set clocks back in the fall.
- ☐ Check windows and doors for weather-tightness and install weather stripping where it's needed.
- ☐ Have furnace professionally inspected.
- ☐ If needed, set traps for rodents.
- ☐ Dust blinds and vacuum curtains throughout your house.
- ☐ Clean kitchen and bathroom cabinets and throw away outdated food, medicine and cosmetics.
- ☐ Inspect and re-caulk any area in kitchen and bathroom where dissimilar materials meet (bathtub-to-tile, toilet-to-floor, sink-to-countertop, countertop-to-backsplash, etc.) and separation has occurred.
- ☐ Inspect all plumbing fixtures for leaks.
- ☐ Check all porcelain fixtures for cracks.
- ☐ _____
- ☐ _____
- ☐ _____
- ☐ _____
- ☐ _____

Winter Home Maintenance

In winter, enjoy energy-efficient warmth and the fruits of your home-maintenance labors. Use this time of the year to thoroughly clean and care for your home's interior while taking a few precautionary measures on the outside.

Outdoor Tasks:

- ☐ Walk around your home's exterior and check the crawl space vents located at the foundation. Close any that are open.
- ☐ Protect your central air conditioning unit with a cover, and remove and store window air conditioners.
- ☐ Clean and store garden tools.
- ☐ Move snow shovels and snow blowers to a convenient spot.
- ☐ _____

☐ _____
☐ _____
☐ _____
☐ _____

Indoor Tasks:

☐ Change or clean furnace filters. Consult manufacturer instructions for your furnace to determine how frequently the filters should be replaced.
☐ Clean kitchen appliances inside and out, including refrigerator coils.
☐ Maintain clean drains by adding one-half-cup baking soda followed by one-half-cup white vinegar. After 10 minutes, flush with boiling water.
☐ _____
☐ _____
☐ _____
☐ _____
☐ _____

See Manufacturer's recommendations for product specific maintenance

Year 9

Spring Home Maintenance

In spring, focus on freshening up your home and protecting your property against the season's strong winds and rains.

Outdoor Tasks:

- ☐ Clean gutters, downspouts, and drains.
- ☐ Inspect roof and chimney for cracks and damage. Inspect all sheet metal – caulk and repaint as needed.
- ☐ Clean deck, patio, porch surfaces, and inspect for surface damage or loose fasteners.
- ☐ Repaint wood surfaces.
- ☐ Check for loose or missing address numbers, or numbers obscured by trees or vines. Clean, paint or polish as needed. Trim or prune any plants covering the numbers or blocking the view from the street. Check numbers at night to verify operation of installed lighting (if any).
- ☐ Lubricate and adjust garage door tracks, rollers, springs, drive chains, screw rods, hinges, door panels, etc. Inspect garage door for scratches or damage, repaint as necessary.
- ☐ Inspect and lubricate gate hinges, latches and locksets. Repaint as needed.
- ☐ Door Chime operates properly.
- ☐ Wash all windows, inside and out.
- ☐ Install screens on windows and doors.
- ☐ Clean outdoor furniture and air out cushions.
- ☐ Service your lawn mower.
- ☐ Irrigation is operational and adjusted to not spray the house.
- ☐ Fertilize your lawn.
- ☐ _____
- ☐ _____
- ☐ _____
- ☐ _____
- ☐ _____

Indoor Tasks:

- ☐ Test smoke and carbon monoxide detectors when you set clocks forward.
- ☐ If your basement has a sump pump, test it by dumping a large bucket of water into the basin of the sump pump. This should activate the sump pump. If it does not switch on or if it's not pumping water, it may need to be serviced by a professional. Also, check for and remove any debris and make sure there are no leaks.
- ☐ Wash and change seasonal bedding.
- ☐ Dust blinds and vacuum curtains throughout your house.
- ☐ Clean kitchen and bathroom cabinets and throw away outdated food, medicine and cosmetics.
- ☐ Inspect and re-caulk any area in kitchen and bathroom where dissimilar materials meet (bathtub-to-tile, toilet-to-floor, sink-to-countertop, etc.) and separation has occurred.
- ☐ Inspect all plumbing fixtures for leaks.
- ☐ Check all porcelain fixtures for cracks.
- ☐ _____
- ☐ _____
- ☐ _____
- ☐ _____
- ☐ _____

Summer Home Maintenance

In summer, complete the following projects to keep your yard lush and your home cool.

Outdoor Tasks:

- ☐ Walk around your home's exterior and slide open crawl space vents at the foundation.
- ☐ Prune trees and shrubs.
- ☐ Inspect and lubricate mailbox hinges, latches, and locks. Paint as needed.
- ☐ Inspect for pests and wood destroying organism activity.

- ☐ Remove lint from dryer exhaust vent with a long, flexible brush.
- ☐ Uncover central air conditioner and install window air conditioners.
- ☐ Inspect gas meter and pipes for rust and corrosion. Remove rust, prep and paint as necessary.
- ☐ _____
- ☐ _____
- ☐ _____
- ☐ _____
- ☐ _____

Indoor Tasks:

- ☐ Change or clean heating, ventilating and air conditioning filters. Consult manufacturer instructions for your furnace to determine whether you need to change filters more frequently. Learn more about choosing a filter.
- ☐ Clean kitchen appliances inside and out, including refrigerator coils.
- ☐ Maintain clean drains by adding a half-cup of baking soda followed by a half-cup of white vinegar. After 10 minutes, flush with boiling water.
- ☐ Drain or flush water heater.
- ☐ _____
- ☐ _____
- ☐ _____
- ☐ _____
- ☐ _____

Fall Home Maintenance

In fall, prepare your home and yard for cooler temperatures, falling leaves and more hours spent indoors.

Outdoor Tasks:

- ☐ Clean gutters and downspouts.
- ☐ Water flows freely away from house and does not pond excessively on patios, decks, porches, etc.
- ☐ Inspect roof and chimney for cracks and damage.
- ☐ Inspect all attic block vents, roof vents and gable end vents to verify that the screens are intact ant that no debris is blocking the screens. Replace any missing or damaged screens.
- ☐ Check for loose or missing address numbers, or numbers obscured by trees or vines. Clean, paint or polish as needed. Trim or prune any plants covering the numbers or blocking the view from the street. Check numbers at night to verify operation of installed lighting (if any)
- ☐ Rake leaves and shred to use as mulch or dispose of them based on local guidelines.
- ☐ Close or install storm windows. Clean tracks and lubricate locking hardware, rollers, etc. Be sure weep holes in windows are clear, and free of debris (if applicable).
- ☐ Remove hoses from spigots and drain and store indoors, coiled and flat.
- ☐ Store outdoor furniture and cushions.
- ☐ Test snow blower and have it professionally serviced if necessary.
- ☐ Rake Leaves
- ☐ _____
- ☐ _____
- ☐ _____
- ☐ _____
- ☐ _____

Indoor Tasks:

- ☐ Test smoke and carbon monoxide detectors when you set clocks back in the fall.
- ☐ Check windows and doors for weather-tightness and install weather stripping where it's needed.
- ☐ Have furnace professionally inspected.
- ☐ If needed, set traps for rodents.
- ☐ Dust blinds and vacuum curtains throughout your house.
- ☐ Clean kitchen and bathroom cabinets and throw away outdated food, medicine and cosmetics.
- ☐ Inspect and re-caulk any area in kitchen and bathroom where dissimilar materials meet (bathtub-to-tile, toilet-to-floor, sink-to-countertop, countertop-to-backsplash, etc.) and separation has occurred.
- ☐ Inspect all plumbing fixtures for leaks.
- ☐ Check all porcelain fixtures for cracks.
- ☐ _____
- ☐ _____
- ☐ _____
- ☐ _____
- ☐ _____

Winter Home Maintenance

In winter, enjoy energy-efficient warmth and the fruits of your home-maintenance labors. Use this time of the year to thoroughly clean and care for your home's interior while taking a few precautionary measures on the outside.

Outdoor Tasks:

- ☐ Walk around your home's exterior and check the crawl space vents located at the foundation. Close any that are open.
- ☐ Protect your central air conditioning unit with a cover, and remove and store window air conditioners.
- ☐ Clean and store garden tools.
- ☐ Move snow shovels and snow blowers to a convenient spot.
- ☐ _____

☐ _____
☐ _____
☐ _____
☐ _____

Indoor Tasks:

☐ Change or clean furnace filters. Consult manufacturer instructions for your furnace to determine how frequently the filters should be replaced.
☐ Clean kitchen appliances inside and out, including refrigerator coils.
☐ Maintain clean drains by adding one-half-cup baking soda followed by one-half-cup white vinegar. After 10 minutes, flush with boiling water.
☐ _____
☐ _____
☐ _____
☐ _____
☐ _____

See Manufacturer's recommendations for product specific maintenance

Year 10

Spring Home Maintenance

In spring, focus on freshening up your home and protecting your property against the season's strong winds and rains.

Outdoor Tasks:

- ☐ Clean gutters, downspouts, and drains.
- ☐ Inspect roof and chimney for cracks and damage. Inspect all sheet metal – caulk and repaint as needed.
- ☐ Clean deck, patio, porch surfaces, and inspect for surface damage or loose fasteners.
- ☐ Touch up peeling or damaged paint.
- ☐ Check for loose or missing address numbers, or numbers obscured by trees or vines. Clean, paint or polish as needed. Trim or prune any plants covering the numbers or blocking the view from the street. Check numbers at night to verify operation of installed lighting (if any).
- ☐ Lubricate and adjust garage door tracks, rollers, springs, drive chains, screw rods, hinges, door panels, etc. Inspect garage door for scratches or damage, repaint as necessary.
- ☐ Inspect and lubricate gate hinges, latches and locksets. Repaint as needed.
- ☐ Door Chime operates properly.
- ☐ Wash all windows, inside and out.
- ☐ Install screens on windows and doors.
- ☐ Clean outdoor furniture and air out cushions.
- ☐ Service your lawn mower.
- ☐ Irrigation is operational and adjusted to not spray the house.
- ☐ Fertilize your lawn.
- ☐ _____
- ☐ _____
- ☐ _____
- ☐ _____
- ☐ _____

Indoor Tasks:

- ☐ Test smoke and carbon monoxide detectors when you set clocks forward.
- ☐ If your basement has a sump pump, test it by dumping a large bucket of water into the basin of the sump pump. This should activate the sump pump. If it does not switch on or if it's not pumping water, it may need to be serviced by a professional. Also, check for and remove any debris and make sure there are no leaks.
- ☐ Wash and change seasonal bedding.
- ☐ Dust blinds and vacuum curtains throughout your house.
- ☐ Clean kitchen and bathroom cabinets and throw away outdated food, medicine and cosmetics.
- ☐ Inspect and re-caulk any area in kitchen and bathroom where dissimilar materials meet (bathtub-to-tile, toilet-to-floor, sink-to-countertop, etc.) and separation has occurred.
- ☐ Inspect all plumbing fixtures for leaks.
- ☐ Check all porcelain fixtures for cracks.
- ☐ _____
- ☐ _____
- ☐ _____
- ☐ _____
- ☐ _____

Summer Home Maintenance

In summer, complete the following projects to keep your yard lush and your home cool.

Outdoor Tasks:

- ☐ Walk around your home's exterior and slide open crawl space vents at the foundation.
- ☐ Prune trees and shrubs.
- ☐ Inspect and lubricate mailbox hinges, latches, and locks. Paint as needed.
- ☐ Inspect for pests and wood destroying organism activity.

- ☐ Remove lint from dryer exhaust vent with a long, flexible brush.
- ☐ Uncover central air conditioner and install window air conditioners.
- ☐ Inspect gas meter and pipes for rust and corrosion. Remove rust, prep and paint as necessary.
- ☐ _____
- ☐ _____
- ☐ _____
- ☐ _____
- ☐ _____

Indoor Tasks:

- ☐ Change or clean heating, ventilating and air conditioning filters. Consult manufacturer instructions for your furnace to determine whether you need to change filters more frequently. Learn more about choosing a filter.
- ☐ Clean kitchen appliances inside and out, including refrigerator coils.
- ☐ Maintain clean drains by adding a half-cup of baking soda followed by a half-cup of white vinegar. After 10 minutes, flush with boiling water.
- ☐ Drain or flush water heater.
- ☐ _____
- ☐ _____
- ☐ _____
- ☐ _____
- ☐ _____

Fall Home Maintenance

In fall, prepare your home and yard for cooler temperatures, falling leaves and more hours spent indoors.

Outdoor Tasks:

- ☐ Clean gutters and downspouts.
- ☐ Water flows freely away from house and does not pond excessively on patios, decks, porches, etc
- ☐ Inspect roof and chimney for cracks and damage.
- ☐ Inspect all attic block vents, roof vents and gable end vents to verify that the screens are intact ant that no debris is blocking the screens. Replace any missing or damaged screens.
- ☐ Check for loose or missing address numbers, or numbers obscured by trees or vines. Clean, paint or polish as needed. Trim or prune any plants covering the numbers or blocking the view from the street. Check numbers at night to verify operation of installed lighting (if any)
- ☐ Rake leaves and shred to use as mulch or dispose of them based on local guidelines.
- ☐ Close or install storm windows. Clean tracks and lubricate locking hardware, rollers, etc. Be sure weep holes in windows are clear, and free of debris (if applicable).
- ☐ Remove hoses from spigots and drain and store indoors, coiled and flat.
- ☐ Store outdoor furniture and cushions.
- ☐ Test snow blower and have it professionally serviced if necessary.
- ☐ Rake Leaves
- ☐ _____
- ☐ _____
- ☐ _____
- ☐ _____
- ☐ _____

Indoor Tasks:

- ☐ Test smoke and carbon monoxide detectors when you set clocks back in the fall.
- ☐ Check windows and doors for weather-tightness and install weather stripping where it's needed.
- ☐ Have furnace professionally inspected.
- ☐ If needed, set traps for rodents.
- ☐ Dust blinds and vacuum curtains throughout your house.
- ☐ Clean kitchen and bathroom cabinets and throw away outdated food, medicine and cosmetics.
- ☐ Inspect and re-caulk any area in kitchen and bathroom where dissimilar materials meet (bathtub-to-tile, toilet-to-floor, sink-to-countertop, countertop-to-backsplash, etc.) and separation has occurred.
- ☐ Inspect all plumbing fixtures for leaks.
- ☐ Check all porcelain fixtures for cracks.
- ☐ _____
- ☐ _____
- ☐ _____
- ☐ _____
- ☐ _____

Winter Home Maintenance

In winter, enjoy energy-efficient warmth and the fruits of your home-maintenance labors. Use this time of the year to thoroughly clean and care for your home's interior while taking a few precautionary measures on the outside.

Outdoor Tasks:

- ☐ Walk around your home's exterior and check the crawl space vents located at the foundation. Close any that are open.
- ☐ Protect your central air conditioning unit with a cover, and remove and store window air conditioners.
- ☐ Clean and store garden tools.
- ☐ Move snow shovels and snow blowers to a convenient spot.
- ☐ _____

- ☐ _____
- ☐ _____
- ☐ _____
- ☐ _____

Indoor Tasks:

- ☐ Change or clean furnace filters. Consult manufacturer instructions for your furnace to determine how frequently the filters should be replaced.
- ☐ Clean kitchen appliances inside and out, including refrigerator coils.
- ☐ Maintain clean drains by adding one-half-cup baking soda followed by one-half-cup white vinegar. After 10 minutes, flush with boiling water.
- ☐ _____
- ☐ _____
- ☐ _____
- ☐ _____
- ☐ _____

See Manufacturer's recommendations for product specific maintenance

BIBLIOGRAPHY AND REFERENCES

American Concrete Institute. (2011). *ACI 318-Building Code Requirements for Structural Concrete.* Farmington Hills, MI.

American Concrete Institute. (2011). *ACI 530- Building Code Requirements for Masonry Structures.* Farmington Hills, MI.

American Forest and Paper Association. (2011) *Wood Frame Construction Manual for One- and Two-Family Dwellings (WFCM).* Leesburg, VA.

American Iron and Steel Institute. (2007). *Standard for Cold-Formed Steel Framing—Prescriptive Method for One - and Two-Family Dwellings (AISI S230).* Washington D.C.

American Society of Heating, Refrigerating and Air-Conditioning Engineers. (2006-2009). *ASHRAE Handbook: Fundamentals.* Atlanta, GA.

Ballast, D. (1994). *Handbook of Construction Tolerances.* McGraw Hill.

Building Industry Association of San Diego County. (1993). *Top 25 Construction Problems and Their Resolution.* Construction Quality Task Force.

California Building Industry Association. (2005). *SB 800, The Homebuilder "FIX IT" Construction Dispute Resolution Law.* Sacramento, CA.

California, State of, Department of Real Estate. (1996). *Operating Cost Manual for Homeowner Association.* Sacramento, CA.

California, State of, Contractor's State License Board. (1982). *Workmanship Guidelines.* Sacramento, CA.

Concrete Committee of San Diego County. (2001). *Concrete Performance Standards and Maintenance guidelines.* San Diego, CA.

Gypsum Association. (2012). *Fire Resistance Design Manual.* Hyattsville, MD.

Hansen, D. & Kardon, R. (2011). *Code Check – Building.* Taunton Press. Newtown, CT.

Hansen, D. & Kardon, R. (2010). *Code Check – Electrical.* Taunton Press. Newtown, CT.

Hansen, D. & Kardon, R. (2011). *Code Check – Plumbing &Mechanical.* Taunton Press. Newtown, CT.

International Code Council. (2007). *California Building Code.* Whittier, CA.

International Code Council. (2007). *California Electrical Code.* Whittier, CA.

International Code Council. (2007). *California Mechanical Code.* Whittier, CA.

International Code Council. (2007). *California Plumbing Code.* Whittier, CA.

International Code Council. (2006-2009). *International Residential Code for One and Two Family Dwellings.* Washington D.C.

International Association of Plumbing & Mechanical Officials. (2009). *Uniform Mechanical Code.* Ontario, CA.

International Association of Plumbing & Mechanical Officials. (2009). *Uniform Plumbing Code.* Ontario, CA.

Journal of Light Construction. (1997). *Troubleshooting Guide to Residential Construction,* Builderburg Group.

NAHM Research Center, Inc. (2001). *Mold in Residential Buildings.* Washington D.C.

National Association of State Contracting Licensing Agencies. (2009). *NASCLA Residential Construction Standards.* Phoenix, AZ.

National Fire Protection Association. (2011). *National Electrical Code.*

National Roofing Contractor's Association. (2007-1009). *NCRA Roofing and Waterproofing Manual.* Vols 1, 2, & 3. Rosemont, IL.

National Wood Flooring Association. (2000). *Problems, Causes and Cures.* Ellisville, MO.

NAHB Home Builder Press. (2005). *Residential Construction Performance Guidelines.* Washington D.C.

New Jersey, State of, Division of Codes and Standards. (2005). *Homeowners booklet,* New Home Warranty Program. NJ.

Reynolds, D. (1998). *Residential & Light Commercial Construction Standards.* R.S. Means, Inc. Kingston, MA.

Sacks, A. (1994). *Residential Water Problems.* NAHM Home Builder Press. Washington, DC.

Structural Building Component Association & Truss Plate Institute. (2006-2013). *Guide to Good Practice for Handling, Installing, Restraining & Bracing of Metal Plate Connected Wood Trusses.*

Tenebaum, D. (1996). *The Complete Idiot's Guide to Trouble Free Home Repair.* Alpha Books. NY.

Truss Plate Institute. (2008). *National Design Standard for Metal Plate Connected Wood Truss Construction.* Alexandria, VA.

ABOUT THE AUTHOR

Ryan Brautovich is an Army veteran with more than 20 years of home construction, home remodeling and building experience who has consulted for Fortune 500 home builders as well as the Top 100 privately held home building companies. He is a custom home builder in California and a California licensed general contractor. Ryan is International Code Council Certified, an International and California Building Inspector as well as an International and California Plumbing Inspector. He is a graduate of Auburn University with degrees in both Accounting and Business Management. He has consulted for the City of Lancaster (CA) Building & Safety Department, K. Hovnanian Homes, Beezer Homes, Pardee Homes, KB Homes, Standard Pacific Homes, American Premiere Homes, Richmond American Homes, DR Horton, and Frontier Homes – just to name a few.

Ryan founded the Construction H.E.L.P. Foundation, a national nonprofit organization, dedicated to advocating for and meeting the needs of individuals who have suffered at the hands of unscrupulous contractors and sub-contractors who simply took advantage of the helpless homeowner in order to make a quick buck – and either didn't finish the project, overcharged or simply took money and didn't perform the work as promised. Over the years, the number of phone calls Ryan received increased dramatically from frustrated and angry homeowners who were desperately seeking help after being ripped off by other contractors. As a result, he founded the Construction H.E.L.P. Foundation, and it's educational assistance program – Home Construction Audit – to provide assistance and education to homeowners. As the founder of the Construction H.E.L.P. Foundation, Ryan has made it the organization's daily mission to return ethics to the home building and home remodeling profession and provide homeowners with the expert help and crucial knowledge they need so that they will never be taken advantage of again.

www.ingramcontent.com/pod-product-compliance
Lightning Source LLC
Chambersburg PA
CBHW020754230426
43665CB00009B/586